YOU HAVE A PET WHAT?!

SUGAR GLIDER

Karen Latchana Kenney

Rourke
Educational Media

rourkeeducationalmedia.com

P9-DYE-476

Before Reading:

Building Academic Vocabulary and Background Knowledge

Before reading a book, it is important to tap into what your child or students already know about the topic. This will help them develop their vocabulary, increase their reading comprehension, and make connections across the curriculum.

1. *Look at the cover of the book. What will this book be about?*
2. *What do you already know about the topic?*
3. *Let's study the Table of Contents. What will you learn about in the book's chapters?*
4. *What would you like to learn about this topic? Do you think you might learn about it from this book? Why or why not?*
5. *Use a reading journal to write about your knowledge of this topic. Record what you already know about the topic and what you hope to learn about the topic.*
6. *Read the book.*
7. *In your reading journal, record what you learned about the topic and your response to the book.*
8. *After reading the book complete the activities below.*

Content Area Vocabulary
Read the list. What do these words mean?

bedding
bond
breeder
exotic
habitat
mammal
marsupial
mealworms
nocturnal
predators
toxic
veterinarian

After Reading:

Comprehension and Extension Activity

After reading the book, work on the following questions with your child or students in order to check their level of reading comprehension and content mastery.

1. *Would a sugar glider be a good pet for you? Explain.* (Text to self connection)
2. *Why do sugar gliders live longer as pets than they do in the wild?* (Infer)
3. *Are people nocturnal? Explain.* (Text to self connection)
4. *What kind of environment does a pet sugar glider need?* (Summarize)
5. *Why are these animals called sugar gliders?* (Asking questions)

Extension Activity

Do you think a sugar glider is a good pet for your family? Before you go out and purchase one, find out the cost. What will it cost to bring home a sugar glider today? Visit a pet store, look on the Internet, or use sales ads to find prices for sugar gliders, a cage, bedding, toys, food, and anything else it might need. How much money do you need to bring it home? How much money will be spent each week on food? If you have another animal, compare the sugar glider to the cost of that animal.

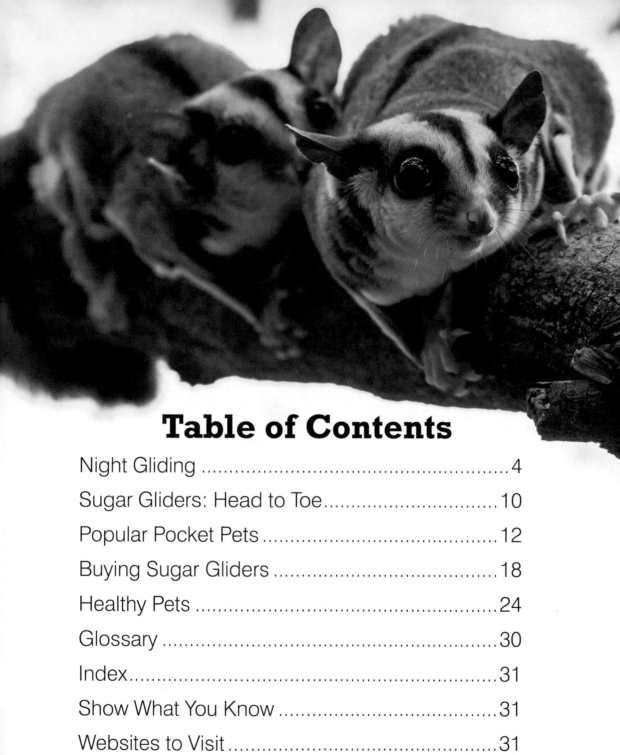

Table of Contents

Night Gliding

Night falls in the forest. The large, round eyes of a sugar glider open. It is time to eat. The **mammal** climbs out from its tree nest. It travels across a limb. Then it jumps!

The sugar glider spreads its four legs. Thin skin stretches from its wrists to its ankles. The skin acts like a kite. It catches the wind. The sugar glider soars from limb to limb. It searches for its next meal. Tree sap and insects are good finds.

A sugar glider is a **marsupial**, like a kangaroo. This is a kind of mammal. Only three kinds of mammals can glide. The sugar glider is one. That's one reason this animal makes a unique pet.

FUN FACT

A sugar glider can glide up to 196 feet (60 meters). That's about half the length of a football field!

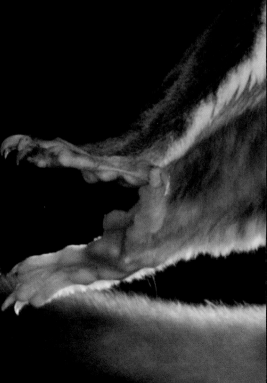

The sugar glider's natural **habitat** is in Australia, Tasmania, Indonesia, and Papua New Guinea. These lands are in the Pacific and Indian Oceans. There, the sugar gliders live in forests. These forests usually have acacia trees.

NORTH PACIFIC OCEAN

INDONESIA

PAPUA NEW GUINEA

Arafura Sea

INDIAN OCEAN

Coral Sea

Great Barrier Reef

AUSTRALIA

SOUTH PACIFIC OCEAN

NEW ZEALAND

Tasman Sea

Tasmania

Sugar gliders are social animals. They live in large groups ranging from 12 to 40 sugar gliders. One or two males lead the group. Females and children, called joeys, join the males. They usually make their nest inside a tree hollow. They line the hollow with leaves and shredded bark.

In the wild, sugar gliders live in trees. They rarely, if ever, touch the ground.

Sugar gliders are **nocturnal**, which means they sleep during the day and are awake during the night.

At night they look for food. They eat both animals and plants.

Females have a pouch for their babies. After just 15 to 17 days, one or two joeys are born. The tiny animals crawl up to the pouch. There they feed and grow more. The joeys leave the pouch between 60 and 70 days later. Soon the mother takes each joey out of the nest. It clings to her back as she looks for food.

FUN FACT

Do you think sugar gliders like sweet foods? They sure do! Tree sap, fruit, and flower nectar are their favorites. They also eat insects and bird eggs.

A glider joey is born as tiny as a cooked grain of rice.

Sugar Gliders: Head to Toe

A sugar glider is a cute little creature. It reaches a length of 10 to 12 inches (25 to 30 centimeters). It weighs just three to five ounces (85 to 142 grams). Its soft fur is gray. A black stripe runs from its eyes to its tail. Its belly is a creamy white.

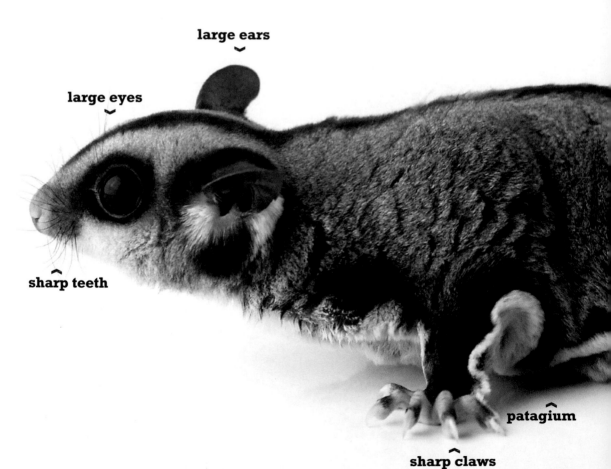

large ears

large eyes

sharp teeth

patagium

sharp claws

The sugar glider has many characteristics that help it survive in the wild.

Sharp Claws: Sharp, curved claws hook into trees as sugar gliders land. The front feet each have five claws. The hind feet have four claws each.

Thumbs: Each foot has a thumb. Sugar gliders use thumbs to grasp onto branches and limbs.

Sharp Teeth: Sugar gliders have between 40 and 46 teeth. Two large teeth are very sharp. They stick out and forward. Sugar gliders use them to chew tree bark.

Large Ears and Eyes: Their large ears can move in all directions. Sugar gliders can hear the quietest sounds. Large eyes stick out from the sugar glider's head. They help it see at night.

Patagium: This is the thin skin that sugar gliders use to glide. It stretches from the wrists to the ankles. When not gliding, the skin ripples at the animal's sides.

Tail: A bushy tail helps sugar gliders balance on tree limbs. During a glide, the tail steers. It controls the direction of the glide.

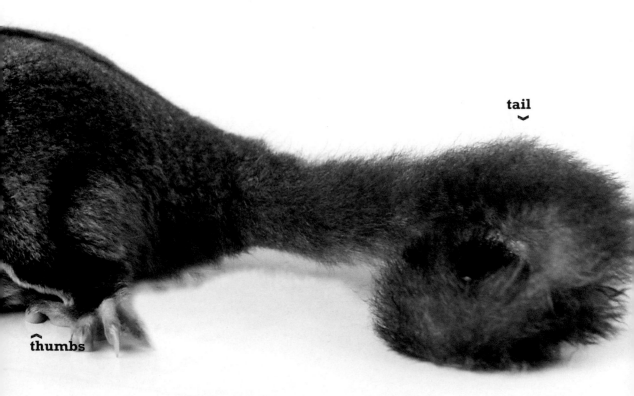

tail

thumbs

Popular Pocket Pets

Sugar gliders love attention and people. They're pretty active, too. Watching them glide and play can be entertaining. An adult can fit in your palm or slip into your pocket. The sugar glider's big eyes and soft fur make it cute and cuddly. This is why people love having them as pets.

FUN FACT

In the wild, sugar gliders live from four to seven years. But as pets, these animals can live up to 15 years. That's about the same lifespan as a cat or dog.

These cute animals are not right for everyone, though. Sugar gliders are not easy pets to care for.

First, they need a lot of attention. Can you take yours out to play every day? If not, can you can afford to care for two sugar gliders? Two sugar gliders can keep each other company.

Sugar gliders also need special food. Will you cut fresh fruit for them every day? Will you keep live insects in the house for them to eat? Knowing how to prepare their food is very important. They can get sick from fruits and vegetables that are not washed well.

a large cage in your home? There are many things to think about before choosing to own a sugar glider.

FUN FACT

Sugar gliders were first brought to the United States as pets in 1993.

Some Owner Risks

Do you have other pets? They may not get along with a sugar glider. A dog might think it is a tasty snack. And birds are the **predators** of sugar gliders in the wild. Pet birds should not be kept near a pet sugar glider.

Playful gliders love to land on houseplants, but some plants are **toxic**. Safe plants include aloe and ferns.

Sugar gliders are expert escape artists. They find ways to get out of their cages. Some head for open toilets. They can easily drown. Others look for open doors and windows. If they escape, they are nearly impossible to catch.

Visit a sugar glider owner before you decide to bring one into your home. Spend some time watching the pet and its owner to decide if a sugar glider is right for you.

Buying Sugar Gliders

So, you've decided to own a sugar glider! How do you get one? Well, first find out if it is legal in your state. Sugar gliders are **exotic** animals. Not every state allows them to be owned as pets. Some states require owners to have permits. Check with your state's fish and wildlife department before you purchase one.

Check this map to see if owning a sugar glider is legal in your state:

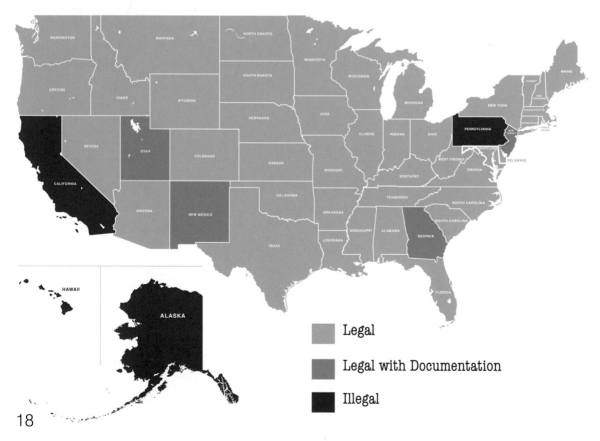

Legal

Legal with Documentation

Illegal

Where you buy a sugar glider is very important. Some breeders do not raise sugar gliders in healthy ways. The United States Department of Agriculture (USDA) gives licenses to good breeders. A licensed **breeder** follows USDA rules. The USDA inspects the breeders. Buying from a licensed breeder helps to make sure you get a healthy pet. In some states, it is only legal to buy sugar gliders from licensed breeders.

 Handle young joeys for at least 30 minutes three or four times a day once their eyes have opened.

Your Pet Sugar Glider

Before you take your new pet glider home, be sure to set up its cage. A sugar glider needs a lot of space to climb and jump. Its cage has to be the right size for it to be happy.

Tall cages are best. The smallest for one to two gliders should be at least 20 inches (50.8 centimeters) wide and deep. It should also be a bit more than 30 inches (76.2 centimeters) tall. Its bars should be about a quarter to a half inch (0.6 to 1.3 centimeters) apart.

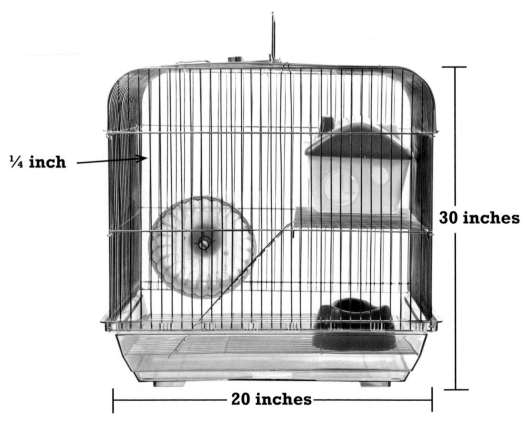

¼ inch

30 inches

20 inches

Keep the air warm. The temperature should be between 70 and 90 degrees Fahrenheit (21 to 32 degrees Celsius). Lay one to two inches (2.5 to 5 centimeters) of **bedding** on the cage floor. Make sure to change the bedding often. Add branches, ladders, and toys. They will keep your pet busy climbing and playing. And don't forget its nest box. That's where your sugar glider can hide and rest during the day.

The Right Diet

Fresh water and a good diet keep sugar gliders healthy. You can't buy bagged sugar glider food. Their food has to be a mix of protein and fresh fruits and vegetables.

For protein, sugar gliders like crickets and **mealworms**. Raw nuts, eggs, cooked plain meats, and tofu are other good proteins. Sugar gliders also eat frozen pinky mice that can be purchased from a pet store.

A variety of fruits and vegetables is best for sugar gliders. Choose three or four types. Some good choices are grapes, apples, carrots, and broccoli. Wash them well and cut everything into chunks.

Feed gliders at night and always remove old food the next day. Then clean out their food dishes and water bottles. It keeps germs from growing and hurting your pet.

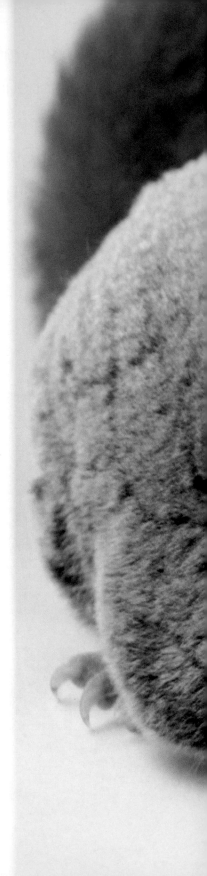

Pet Pointers

Sugar gliders need about 24 percent protein in their diets. That works out to about one tablespoon of protein each day. They also need 1/4 to 1/3 cup of fruit and vegetables each day.

Healthy Pets

Sometimes sugar gliders get sick. They might get mites or ticks. They might have problems with their stools. Or they might gain too much weight. Carefully checking their diet helps. Keeping their cages very clean is important too. Sugar gliders mostly groom themselves, but you may need to trim their nails. They can get pretty sharp!

If your sugar glider does get sick, take it to a **veterinarian**. Not all veterinarians treat exotic animals. Ask the breeder who sold you your sugar glider. They can likely suggest someone to you.

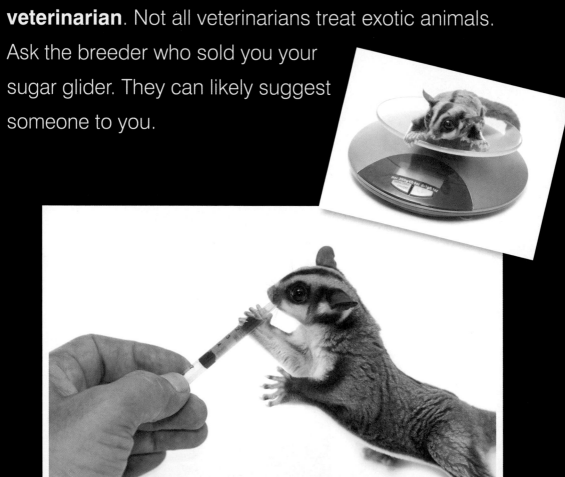

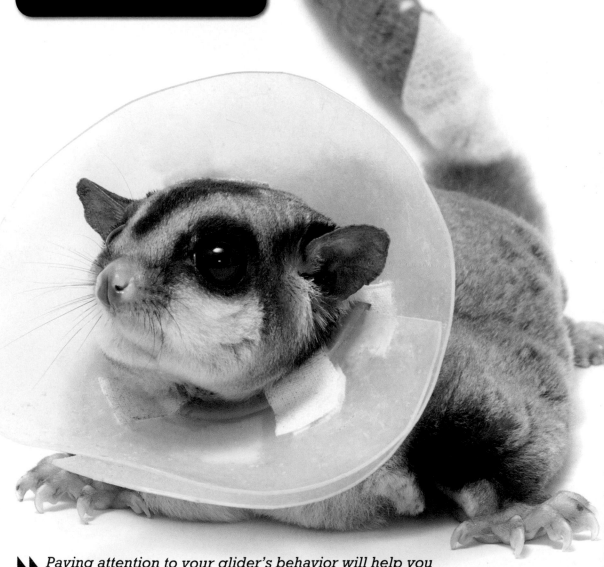

Pet Pointers

Signs of a sick glider:

- weight loss
- hair loss
- a dirty bottom
- dragging its hind legs
- wheezy breathing
- open wounds

Paying attention to your glider's behavior will help you determine if it is happy and healthy.

Bonding and Attention

A new pet sugar glider needs time to **bond** with its owner. This is very important. Once bonded, a sugar glider shows love for its owner.

Let your pet settle into its new home for a few days. Give it a sock or T-shirt that has your scent so it can get used to your smell. Then slowly try to pet your glider. Slip it into your pocket. Walk around with it. Soon the glider will come out. It will crawl on you, and it will start to play.

Sugar gliders love attention. They need two to four hours each night. Let your pet out to play, spend time with you, and discover its new surroundings.

Sweet Sugar Gliders

Watch a pet sugar glider. It plays, climbs, and glides. Its soft fur and big eyes make it cute and cuddly. Its bond with its owner makes it a loving pet. Care for it well. Give it your time and attention. Your pet sugar glider could be your next best friend!

Things to Think About if You Want a Pet Sugar Glider

- Pet sugar gliders live up to 15 years.
- They need two to four hours of attention each night.
- They eat foods that take time to prepare. Fresh fruit and vegetables may also be costly.
- Their cages need to be kept very clean.
- Their cages may take up a lot of space in your home.
- Regular veterinarians may not be able to care for sugar gliders.

Glossary

bedding (BED-ing): material used for animals to cushion their bodies and absorb smells and wetness

bond (BOND): to form a close connection

breeder (BREED-ur): a person who keeps, mates, and sells animals

exotic (eg-ZOT-ic): in animals, one that is native to another country

habitat (HAB-uh-tat): the place in nature where an animal or plant lives

mammal (MAM-uhl): a warm-blooded animal with a spine, whose females produce milk for their young

marsupial (mar-SOO-pee-uhl): a type of mammal, such as a kangaroo or sugar glider, whose females have pouches in which their young grow and develop

mealworms (MEEL-wurmz): the larva of beetles

nocturnal (nok-TUR-nuhl): to be active at night

predators (PRED-uh-turz): an animal that hunts other animals for food

toxic (TOK-sic): poisonous

veterinarian (vet-ur-uh-NER-ee-uhn): a doctor who treats sick animals

Index

Show What You Know

1. How do sugar gliders glide?

2. What are baby sugar gliders called?

3. When are sugar gliders awake?

4. What do pet sugar gliders eat?

5. Who should you buy a pet sugar glider from?

Websites to Visit

animaldiversity.org/accounts/Petaurus_breviceps

video.nationalgeographic.com/video/sugar_glider?source=relatedvideo

www.wildlife.org.au/wildlife/speciesprofile/mammals/gliders/sugar_glider.html

About the Author

Karen Latchana Kenney is the author of more than 100 books for children. She's written about all kinds of animals—from the tiny bee hummingbird to the spiny sea urchin. Kenney lives and works in Minneapolis, Minnesota.

Meet The Author!
www.meetREMauthors.com

www.rourkeeducationalmedia.com

PHOTO CREDITS: Cover: ©NuntapobKaewrvang; title page: ©pigphoto; page 3: ©rujithai; page4-5, page 9: ©corbis; page6: ©roripond; page 7: ©Belinda Wright; page8, page 12-13, page 19 (bottom), page 27: ©eugenesergeev; page 10-11: ©eve_eveolgenius; page 14: ©Sevendeman; page 15 (top): ©Farinoza; page 15 (middle): ©Mr. Suttipan Yakham; page 15(bottom): ©Chaturonk; page 16 (top): ©Oktay Ortakcioglu; page 16 (bottom): ©Ulga; page 17 (top): ©antpkr; page 17 (bottom): ©Petr Novotny; page 19 (top): Wikipedia; page 20: ©Brazhnykov Andriy; page 21: © Carmelka; page 23: ©Suchat Siriboot; page 24 (top and bottom), page 25, page 30: ©Praisang; page 28 (top): ©Kimberrywood; page 28 (bottom), page 29: ©GlobalP

Edited by: Keli Sipperley

Cover design and Interior design by: Rhea Magaro

Library of Congress PCN Data

Sugar Glider / Karen Latchana Kenney
 (You Have a Pet What?!)
  ISBN 978-1-63430-436-8 (hard cover)
  ISBN 978-1-63430-536-5 (soft cover)
  ISBN 978-1-63430-625-6 (e-Book)
Library of Congress Control Number: 2015931859

Printed in the United States of America, North Mankato, Minnesota

Also Available as: